The
Science
of
Mindfulness

Raza Imam

Table of Contents

How I Wrote This Book

"Give me a one-page bullet-list of exactly what I should do. That's worth more to me than a stack of books that I have to dig through to get to the good stuff. I may give you 50 bucks for the books. But I'll pay you $5,000 for the one page."

That's a quote from Alwyn Cosgrove, a world-famous strength coach and entrepreneur.

I love it because it's how I like to write my books.

I COULD write a 250 page book on every single facet of mindfulness.

But that would be overkill.

I find that rather than stuffing my books with tons of theory, my readers appreciate the "cliff" notes.

They want to know why something works, and how to do it.

In this short book, I've given you everything you need to know about mindfulness.

I discuss how it benefits you and I share studies and research to back it up.

But this isn't a dry, technical, research book.

This book is short, and that's for a reason.

I want to convince you that this stuff works, show you why it works, and then give you 100% actionable content, not a bunch of fluff and theory.

Sure I give practical examples to prove my point.

Yes I give you specific action items to do and I explain why.

Of course I tell you exactly how to implement these steps to get the best results.

But I worked *ruthlessly* to keep this book short and sweet.

So remember to **take action** - because that's *all* that matters.

If you have any questions, you can always email me at razasimam@outlook.com

Introduction

Distraction.

Stress.

Worry.

Frustration.

Anxiety.

Restlessness.

Fatigue.

Depression.

It's sad to say, but these feelings are commonplace of daily life.

The daily grind has us so scared, stressed, and anxious, that we move from one task to another like drones controlled by a shadowy puppet master.

No wonder we're so unfocused, so unproductive, and worst of all, so disconnected from each other.

But there is a silver lining.

By simply living more mindfully, that is, being aware of our surroundings, noticing them, and appreciating them, we can start to regain a sense of calm, and inner peace, and hope… in just a few minutes a day.

Mindfulness as a concept has been around for centuries, but over the past 30 years, it has take the Western world by storm.

Precisely because Western, industrialized countries are so obsessed with production and consumption, that we give ourselves very little time to actually enjoy life.

So we're constantly stressed and disconnected from the people around us.

Does the following scenario sound familiar?

Your alarm wakes you up in the morning.

You go to the bathroom and check your email and scroll through Facebook, Instagram, and the news.

You check your text messages and reply to any you missed the night before.

Half awake, you jump into the shower, then run out and get dressed, dry your hair, shave.

You run out the door, only to be met with gridlocked traffic.

You sit in traffic for an hour, hoping you're on time to a job that you don't like.

Have you eaten breakfast?

Have you even brushed your teeth?

"Oh crap", you think to yourself "did I forget to brush my teeth this morning???"

You rush to the breakroom to grab a cup of coffee, wondering how you're going to get a toothbrush.

On the way back to your desk, you spill coffee on your shirt.

And it's not even 8:30 yet.

If you're tired of this stressed, hectic life, there is an alternative.

And it starts with being mindful.

As simple as it sounds, it's a proven, safe, reliable way to reduce anxiety and stress, treat depression (or symptoms of depression), improve your ability to think and focus, and live a more satisfying life.

Sound too good to be true?

It's not.

And I'm going to prove it in this book.

Many of you are no doubt familiar with the concept of mindfulness (after all, you are currently reading a book on the topic, so you may have done some research on the matter).

However, many more have probably never heard of mindfulness before because, while it is growing in popularity, it is still not talked about all that much in the mainstream media.

This chapter is intended to serve as an introduction to the Science of Mindfulness. Every question you have about mindfulness will be answered.

What is mindfulness?

Explaining mindfulness is not easy, because there are so many definitions.

The most basic dictionary definition (from Merriam-Webster) defines mindfulness as: "the practice of maintaining a nonjudgmental state of heightened or complete awareness of one's thoughts, emotions, or experiences on a moment-to-moment basis."

Obviously, that's not a very helpful definition, because it doesn't convey what mindfulness *does* for you.

Let's try another, more meaningful definition of mindfulness.

Jon Kabat-Zinn, one of the men responsible for helping to popularize mindfulness in the 1990s, defined mindfulness as: "Mindfulness means paying attention in a particular way: on purpose, in the present moment, and nonjudgmentally."

This is a far more helpful and useful definition.

If you are still struggling with understanding what mindfulness is, let me explain it this way. Stop whatever you're doing, sit down for a minute, and just stop thinking about everything.

Completely quiet your mind, don't think about family problems, don't think about problems with at work, don't think about financial problems.

Just sit and think of nothing.

It's a lot harder than it seems, isn't it?

You try to quiet your mind and yet, problems that you worry about keep creeping into your mind.

What mindfulness attempts to do is to help you learn to quiet your mind.

Mindfulness is very closely related to several other practices that you are probably more familiar with, such as yoga, meditation and tai chi.

Activities such as these help you cultivate mindfulness and put 100% of your focus on what you're doing.

Meditation especially helps you to learn how to clear your mind. It helps you cultivate mindfulness because of its slow, deliberate pace.

Things like intense exercise, while healthy for your body, are a bit too fast paced to really help you cultivate a state of mindfulness.

Meditation is very slow and very calming, which makes it ideal for cultivating mindfulness.

Because meditation is so connected to mindfulness, this book will feature a chapter which explains more about meditation and how one should go about doing it properly.

Mindfulness and the practice of cultivating it can essentially be divided into four parts:

1). Focusing

If you have ever meditated before, then you know that an important part of meditation is focusing all your attention on a single activity, especially your breathing.

Part of developing mindfulness involves learning how to focus all your attention on a single activity. This usually means focusing all your attention on breathing.

2). Scanning

An important part of developing mindfulness is learning to "scan things." In other words, you need to learn to think about the individual parts of something as opposed to thinking about it as a whole. For example, let's look at a common mindfulness-building activity called body scanning.

Body scanning is an activity described by John Kabat-Zinn, a man who will be discussed in more detail later. When you do a body scan, you essentially focus on various parts of your body. So, you may focus on your toes, then slowly work your way upwards, devoting your full attention to different parts of your body.

The idea behind this is to essentially train your mind to be able to focus on things. It also trains your mind to be able to switch its focus easily. For example, you may start out focusing on your toes, but then you can quickly move onto something bigger, like your arms, then you move back to a smaller part of your body.

As you can see, this activity forces you to take something that you would normally think of as a whole (your body) and think about its individual parts (your fingers, toes, etc.).

3). Changing Perspectives

An important part of cultivating mindfulness is learning how to change one's perspective on life. When you are dealing with the stresses and hardships of day-to-day life, it's too easy to lose sight of yourself and what's important. Mindfulness helps you realize that you can persevere through hardship.

It sounds odd, but trust me when I say that it works.

4). Control Over Your Emotions

Last, but not least, is the importance of emotional control. In stressful times, it is easy to let your emotions get the better of you. Thus, it is important to learn how to control your emotions and how to react to emotional situations. This will lead to you making smarter decisions in stressful situations when others let their emotions get the better of them.

Why is it important?

People today live extremely hectic lives. Between family and work obligations, everyone is on the go constantly.

Plus, everyone has their own set of unique problems that stress them out.

Now there's nothing wrong with being stressed out at times, stress can be a great motivator and it can help you focus.

The problem is that in the hustle and bustle of regular life, people have forgotten to take a few moments each day for a bit of reflection and relaxation.

This is bad, to say the least.

When stress starts to build up, it can cause real health problems, including headaches, stomach aches, muscle pains, depression, fatigue, insomnia, and much worse.

People try various methods to get rid of stress from constructive things like working out, journaling, volunteering to destructive things like drugs, alcohol, social isolation, etc.

This is where mindfulness comes in to play. It's an effective, safe, and empowering way to deal with the stresses of daily life.

In addition to its various other benefits (all of which you will learn about in this book), mindfulness is a very effective way of reducing stress.

How did mindfulness develop?

The idea of mindfulness is very old. The term "mindfulness" comes from the word *Sati*, which is an important part of Buddhist philosophy that stretches back thousands of years.

In the modern day, the practice of mindfulness was introduced to the West in 1979 when John Kabat-Zinn, a professor of medicine at the University of Massachusetts Medical School pioneered what he called "mindfulness-based stress reduction" (MBSR for short).

MBSR uses various techniques to increase one's mindfulness, which in turn causes a reduction in stress levels. MBSR started becoming very popular in the 1990s, to the point where various organizations have adopted MBSR to help deal with stress levels.

For example, the famous food company, General Mills, has adopted MBSR to help its employees manage their stress levels (they even have rooms set aside for meditation and reflection). Even the US Marine Corps is looking into adopting MBSR to help soldiers deal with combat stress. If MBSR is useful enough for major companies and respected organizations, then it will be useful for you.

The benefits of mindfulness

Alright, so now that we all have a clear understanding of what mindfulness is and how it developed, it is time to move onto discussing what the benefits of mindfulness are.

That is what the majority of this book will be devoted to.

To be clear, this is not speculation.

Every benefit listed in this book is backed up by actual scientific research. It may be tempting to dismiss things like mindfulness and MBSR as new-age mumbo-jumbo, they are both backed up by many scientific studies.

In the rest of this book, you will learn how mindfulness and MSBR can be used to reduce stress, improve your cognitive abilities, and even do miraculous things like make you healthier.

Chapter 1: How to Instantly Melt Stress and Worry Using Mindfulness

One of the biggest benefits of mindfulness is stress reduction.

That's probably why the concept of mindfulness is so popular among, Westernized, urbanized, industrialized countries.

With the combo of gridlocked traffic, concrete surroundings, noise pollution, lack of exercise, poor sleep, and the constant hum of electronics, from cell phones, to computer monitors, to televisions, it's no wonder we're wound so tight.

So, if you have read the introduction, then you probably picked up that one of the main benefits of cultivating mindfulness is that it can help you deal with stress. While this isn't the only benefit, it certainly is one of the main ones; and it is certainly one of the most well-researched benefits.

In this chapter, we are going to fully explore why mindfulness and MBSR can be used to reduce stress levels.

As mentioned earlier, moderate amounts of stress are not bad for you. In fact, a moderate amount of stress is good for you, it keeps you focused on a single task and it acts as a good motivator.

But if you always feel like you're stressed, and start to feel a sense of panic and hopelessness, it can start to affect your health, draining you of energy, making you feel lethargic, or preventing you from sleeping and eating properly.

Mindfulness has been proven to fight the debilitating effects of stress. This has been proven time and time again in various scientific studies.

One example of such a study was published in the *Journal of Research in Personality*, which is a scientific journal run by the Dutch Company Elsevier. In this study, participants were asked to practice MBSR techniques during particularly stressful moments. The goal was to see how effective these techniques were at reducing the impact of the stressful event and to see how MBSR techniques improved the person's ability to respond to the stressful event. The study involved over a 140 people and was extremely positive. Most of the participants reported that MBSR techniques did improve their ability to respond to the stressful event.

Now that's just one study, but there are much more out there.

Let's take a look at one more general study before moving on. A study published in the well-respected medical journal *Health Psychology* analyzed the connection between mindfulness and the hormone cortisol. Cortisol is a nasty little stress hormone and is released by the body when you are in stressful situations. Cortisol shuts down the digestive process, causes bone and muscle loss, accelerates aging, loss of focus, difficulty sleeping, and a host of other undesirable processes. The study actually found that mindfulness reduced cortisol levels in the subjects tested. To quote the study: "large increases in mindfulness were associated with decreases in cortisol." This pretty clearly shows that mindfulness is effective at decreasing general stress levels.

So far, we have talked primarily about general stress levels, but what about people who suffer conditions that increase their stress levels? For example, how well does mindfulness work on people who suffer from an actual anxiety disorder?

Well, researchers conducted a study to see how effective mindfulness would be at helping people who suffer from generalized anxiety disorder. Sufferers of this disorder have unbearable amounts of anxiety and can often struggle at mundane tasks due to the sheer amount of anxiety that they have.

The study, which was published in the *Journal of Clinical Psychiatry* and which involved the Massachusetts General Hospital, showed that yes, mindfulness can help people suffering from generalized anxiety disorder. The study involved 93 people who suffer from generalized anxiety disorder and it found that patients who participated in MBSR sessions were significantly less anxious than those patients who did not participate. More amazingly, the study found that MBSR is so powerful, that even just one session produced significant reductions in anxiety levels.

If you want further proof of the power of mindfulness, then you only need to look at the ability of MBSR to help people suffering from restless leg syndrome. Sufferers of this condition, suffer from a strong, uncontrollable desire to move their legs, even when they are sleeping. Although the condition may sound mild, people who suffer from it often have restless nights and next to no energy. Although there are ways to help live with the syndrome, there is no known cure.

So, researchers are constantly looking for new ways to help people who suffer from restless leg syndrome. A 2016 study done by the Catholic University of Australia evaluated 8 patients with restless leg syndrome. They were put through a 6-week MBSR program and afterward were questioned about their experiences and thoughts. All the patients who participated in the program reported that they experienced a noticeable improvement in their restless leg syndrome after going through the MBSR program. More specifically, the patients reported that their quality of life was improved and that they slept better.

Now, I have three kids, and I can tell you that raising kids is stressful.

Getting to fall asleep. Getting them to stay asleep. Getting them to eat. Getting them to take a bath. Making sure they do their homework. Making sure they put away their clothes and toys. Makings sure they're nice to their siblings.

It's hard work and causes a LOT of stress.

Parents, especially new ones, often find themselves at their wit's end when dealing with their kids. This is bad for both parties involved. Parents who are stressed out all the time will be less effective. And nobody wants that.

Likewise, the kids suffer because they pick up on their parents being stressed, and sometimes act out because of it.

A 2017 study done by the American Psychological Association looked at whether mindfulness could be used to help stressed-out parents. As part of the study, various parents were given an 8-week course in mindfulness. The results showed 4 important things:

1) The parents became better at controlling their emotions in intense situations

2) The parents were more compassionate towards their children

3) The parents were more consistent in how they parented and in how they approached their children

4) There was a noticeable improved in the parent-child relationship.

Parenting is an extremely tough and stressful job, but even with something as tough as parenting, mindfulness is still incredibly useful, as this study demonstrates.

We talked about earlier how the Marine Corps is considering adopting mindfulness training to help soldiers deal with stress. Well, there is actually evidence to suggest that MBSR is useful in combating PTSD.

A 2017 study found that former soldiers suffering from PTSD reported massive improvements after undergoing a mindfulness training course. Now it is well-known that many combat veterans suffer from PTSD, but plenty of other people in traumatic occupations are at risk of developing PTSD. Firefighters, law enforcement officials, and many others are all at risk. And the simple practice of mindfulness can help with all of this.

14

But, before we move on, there is one more thing I want to discuss and that is the usefulness of mindfulness for dealing with work-related stress.

For many of us, our job is a major of stress and anxiety. This is especially true for those who work in very intense jobs, such as doctors, police officers, etc. or jobs with tight deadlines and overbearing managers. Studies have shown that mindfulness and MBSR are extremely helpful for people in these high-stress job environments.

A 2016 study published in the journal *Stress & Health* found that there was a large body of evidence to suggest that mindfulness could be of great use to healthcare professionals as a method for reducing stress.

A similar study, also done in 2016, found that when police officers engaged in MBSR, they experienced reduced organizational and operational stress, as well as reduced anger levels.

There is a great potential for mindfulness to help reduce work-related stress in all occupations. If mindfulness and MBSR can reduce the stress levels of people working in law enforcement and in medical care, then it is no doubt useful for reducing stress in any profession that you can think of. So, no matter what profession you work in, if it is causing you unbearable amounts of stress, then you may find mindfulness useful.

In this chapter, you have learned why mindfulness is such an effective way to combat stress.

Furthermore, you've seen how it does more than just fight against general stress, it also fights against anxiety disorders, job-related stress, parenting-related stress, and much more. If you find that you have a large amount of stress in your life and that you are struggling to combat it, then you should seriously consider looking into cultivating mindfulness and MBSR; for some, it can be a lifesaver.

Chapter 2: How to Effortlessly Burn Fat, Fight Disease, and Reduce Chronic Pain Using Mindfulness

Alright, so far, we have covered how mindfulness can help relieve stress. While that is certainly a very important function of mindfulness, it can also have actual, tangible physical benefits as well.

There is a large body of research that suggests that mindfulness can actually make you physically healthier. There are studies that suggest, among other things, that mindfulness can actually lead to a healthier immune system, less soreness, and less inflammation in your body. It may sound wild at first, after all, how could the simple process of quieting your mind do so much good for your body? But, it is all completely backed up by reputable scientific studies.

Let's start first with looking at what mindfulness can do for your immune system. We all hate getting sick, nobody likes sitting in bed with a head cold, a flu, or a fever.

Reportedly, one of the best ways of avoiding getting sick is vaccinations, but even that will only get you so far. Even with vaccines, you still need a strong immune system to avoid getting sick. That's where mindfulness comes in.

Believe it or not, studies do show that mindfulness and MBSR do help improve your body's immune system. A 2009 study published in the scientific journal, *Psychoneuroendocrinology,* took a group of 61 healthy adults and split them into 2 groups. Both groups were given identical vaccines, but only one group was given a 6-week session of mindfulness training to go along with it. The results of the study, as you can probably guess, showed that the group that was given both vaccines and MBSR were better off than the group that just got vaccinated. The group that received both seemed to have more antibodies in their system (which indicates that their immune system was working more efficiently). Likewise, the group that received both also seemed to just take to the vaccination better than the group that only received the vaccination. This was not just some one-off study either, there are other studies that back up these findings.

For example, a study was done in 2003 also found that those who took both vaccinations and MBSR had better results and more efficient immune systems than those who only took vaccinations.

What exactly is it about mindfulness that helps your immune system? Experts are unsure, as there are a bunch of factors at work. However, the most likely reason why mindfulness and MBSR seem to help your immune system is due to the fact that it relieves stress.

See, most of us are familiar with how stress can cause back pain, muscle pain, headaches, and stomach aches, but stress can actually do a lot of damage to various important parts of your body, including your immune system.

Now, this is not saying that if you are a bit stressed out, that you are suddenly going to get sick. Rather, being stressed out constantly makes your immune system less efficient and less able to beat off viruses. So, by helping to relieve stress, mindfulness can actually help you fight off sickness and keep you healthy.

Do you notice that you are constantly getting sick? Do you notice that it seems like every couple of weeks you are developing the flu, a cold, or some other minor virus? If so, it is possible that this is due to stress compromising your immune system. This is especially true if you work in an office environment. The mixture of stress and large amounts of employees in close quarters contributes to an environment where it's really easy to get sick. If this sounds familiar, then you should seriously look into MBSR, not only will it make you less stressed out, it will also make you healthier overall.

Mindfulness and meditation are so powerful that they can even reduce the amount of pain you feel. Sound far fetched? Well read on…

The connection between mindfulness and pain was the subject of a 2011 study published in the *Journal of Neuroscience*. The study found that mindfulness training and meditation could reduce "pain unpleasantness" by close to 60%. Likewise, the study also found that "pain intensity ratings" could be reduced by up to 40%.

Impressive if you ask me.

This is not the only study to show this link either, at least 3 separate past studies have backed up these findings. These findings are especially useful for those who suffer from chronic pain. People who regularly deal with neck pain, back pain, or any other kind of muscle pain would benefit from these findings. Similarly, those with conditions that cause pain, such as arthritis, would also very much benefit from these findings.

Usually, people with chronic pain are reduced to taking pain medications or simply suffering in silence. However, pain medications can have some nasty side effects (the biggest one being that many prescription pain medications are very easy to get addicted to and were pushed by big pharma… but that's a topic for another day). Cultivating mindfulness and regular meditation have no nasty side effects and thus will be very useful for people suffering from chronic pain medications.

Now, you may be curious as to how mindfulness can help reduce feelings of pain. Well, unlike with your immune system, the answer has nothing to do with stress. Rather, the reason mindfulness can help reduce pain is due to the fact that mindfulness actually alters the way your brain works.

I love reading (and writing) about this stuff!

See, since mindfulness helps you clear your mind, it also changes what your mind focuses on. So, when you meditate or engage in a body scan, your mind focuses on other things, which reduces the sensation of pain. The pain is still there, but your mind is focused on other things. Now, I could keep going on and explain how the various parts of the brain work and how pain works, but that's probably not necessary. All you need to understand is that mindfulness changes how your brain works, which makes you feel less chronic pain. But, it is also important to note that there are a few caveats… (bummer)

First off, this only works long-term or chronic pain, you do not just undergo mindfulness training and suddenly become impervious to pain. Secondly, this benefit does not come overnight, it will take a continuous regimen of cultivating mindfulness to actually reduce your feelings of pain.

So there is some work involved, but it's doable. They key is to control your emotional state surrounding pain. Don't fear it because the anticipation makes it worse. The key is to accept it and allow yourself to focus on something else.

Finally, let's talk about inflammation. Many of you out there either suffer from inflammation or know relatives who do (this is especially true because inflammation tends to occur more often in older people).

Inflammation is how your body responds to various kinds of stimuli like stress, a poor diet, and even exercise. The effects of chronic inflammation can be difficult to deal with, because it causes major problems over time.

That is where mindfulness and MBSR come into play. A 2013 study compared an MBSR program to a HEP program (HEP is short for Health Enhancement Program). The results showed that:

"however, MBSR training resulted in a significantly smaller post-stress inflammatory response compared to HEP, despite equivalent levels of stress hormones."

Even more interestingly, the study showed that activities that reduce emotional reactivity would also be helpful for reducing stress-induced inflammation. Basically, what the study said was that cultivating mindfulness, because it calms your mind and reduces stress levels, your body is better able to defend against things that cause chronic inflammation.

This chapter has shown how mindfulness and MBSR do not just have benefits for your mind, they actually benefit you physically.

This is very important to keep in mind. A lot of people wrongly dismiss things like mindfulness because they assume it does not have any real physical benefits.

I used to think that too… so I know how you feel!

But, as I've shown in this chapter, there is real scientific evidence that shows that mindfulness can reduce feelings of pain, reduce inflammation, and even improve your immune system.

These are very real physical benefits and I could keep going on and on about the various physical benefits associated with mindfulness, but that would be worthy of a book of its own.

The idea was to give you a brief snapshot of the physical benefits of cultivating mindfulness so that you believe in it and DO it.

Interested in Getting Healthier?

Check out my #1 bestseller

"**The Science of Getting Ripped**: Proven Diet Hacks and Workout Tricks to Build Muscle and Burn Fat in Half the Time"

http://a.co/fHoBhEm

or

"**The Home Workout Handbook**: Proven Workouts to Get Lean and Ripped in 30 Minutes a Day"

http://a.co/e2a7VcQ

Chapter 3: How to Easily Build Mental Toughness, Fight Depression, and Become Unstoppable Using Mindfulness

It goes without saying that we all suffer from bouts of sadness and depression at some point in our life.

People often carry on with their lives despite having persistent feelings of depression or sadness. But, numerous studies have consistently shown that carrying around feelings of depression or sadness can lead to some very real consequences.

In fact, I heard an interesting story from fitness YouTuber Brandon Carter. For those who don't know, Brandon Carter has tens of millions of YouTube views. He's a chiseled, muscular, New York City trainer turned entrepreneur. He used his fan base on YouTube to create a supplement company. He's loud, outspoken, opinionated, and funny.

Most people see his tattoos, big biceps, and potty mouth and think of him as a brain-dead bonehead.

But when you peel the onion, you learn a lot more.

For example, he's an avid reader, often reading a book (or more) a week.

That he's logged everything he's eaten for the past several years - and has the food journals to prove it.

That his father shot himself in the head.

That part struck me.

What was even more striking is how often Brandon feels like killing himself.

It's shocking really.

Why would a muscular, attractive, popular, famous, wealthy young man regularly think of ending his own life?

Perhaps it's because depression is hereditary and he inherited it from his father.

Maybe because the pressure of being in the public eye is too much for him to bear.

Whatever the reason, he said the #1 reason he hasn't killed himself is because of meditation (and obviously mindfulness).

So don't underestimate this stuff - it's that powerful.

Think about it, people with negative outlooks on life often struggle at work and they struggle in their personal life. Not to mention the fact that negative feelings can actually hurt your health. People with negative outlooks will struggle to exercise regularly or eat healthy on a regular basis.

The opposite is true as well. People with positive outlooks on life tend to succeed in every aspect of their life. They do well in their career (or if they don't have a career, they do much better at finding one). They do well in their social life and are able to make friends more easily than someone with a negative outlook. And a positive outlook leads to a person living a longer, healthier life.

So, what does any of this have to do with mindfulness? Well, it's all well and good to say to someone that they should adopt a more positive outlook on life. But, the **reality** is that shaking negative feelings can be *difficult*.

Many people resort to antidepressants to deal with lingering depression issues, and even that isn't **guaranteed** to work.

Mindfulness on the other hand, can both help people conquer feelings of depression and sadness, while at the same time actually helping them develop a more positive outlook on life.

So, let's start by talking about depression, shall we?

Depression is a skyrocketing problem in the modern world. Researchers are not exactly sure why, but studies suggest that the changing lifestyles of urban dwellers combined with the fast pace of modern life may contribute to rising depression levels.

Who knows… but we should all care.

Regardless of why depression is more common, the simple fact is that is becoming a bigger issue, especially in affluent, industrialized countries.

Big pharma is definitely capitalizing on the trend and offering more and more antidepressants - without spending an equal amount of time and money on treating the problem at its root.

But I digress…

The point is that many antidepressants carry negative side effects that can actually worsen the symptoms of depression. Just listen to drug commercials!

Here's a funny story to illustrate how big pharma is actually perpetuating problems, not solving them. A friend of mine was struggling with vertigo, which was causing nausea. The doctor prescribed a medication to treat nausea and vertigo, but guess what a potential side effect was…. nausea!

On top of that, certain antidepressants can be highly addictive.

If you're thinking to yourself "*there **has** to be a better way*", there is; mindfulness.

A 2004 study published in the journal *Cognitive Therapy and Research* took a group of patients who suffered from depression and who had tendencies to engage in ruminative thinking. The patients were asked to participate in an 8-week course based around mindfulness. They engaged in standard MBSR (for those who may have forgotten, this stands for mindfulness-based stress reduction). The results of the study showed that developing mindfulness did help the patients with their depression and their tendency to engage in ruminative thinking - ruminative thinking is a term used by psychologists to refer to many people's tendency to essentially dwell on negative emotional experiences As you can imagine, this tendency does not help those who are already suffering from depression.

If you're curious as to why developing mindfulness is able to help with depression and ruminative thinking, all you need to do is think back to the last chapter. Remember how we talked about how mindfulness can actually shape the way your brain works?

Well, the same thing is happening here.

Developing mindfulness actually changes your brain activity and shifts the way your brain works, both of which help minimize the effects of depression and ruminative thinking.

We should also consider the impact of stress management. We've already established, mindfulness can help people deal with stress. Well, there is a well-known connection between stress and depression.

These two little incestuous parasites actually feed off each other.

Stress can make a person's depression worse and depression can make a person already suffering from extreme stress even more stressed out. So, by helping people to deal with their stress, mindfulness and MBSR can actually also help people with depression as well.

Let's switch gears and talk about how mindfulness can help you adopt a more positive outlook on life. Evidence has consistently shown that cultivating mindfulness produces positive emotions.

Awesome!

Furthermore, mindfulness also helps keep your negative emotions in check.

Double awesome!

As a book published by Oxford University in 2014 said: *"Evidence suggests that dispositional mindfulness is associated with higher levels of positive emotion and lower levels of negative emotion."* Other studies have backed up these findings as well.

For example, a famous 2011 study done by Doctor B. L. Frederickson showed that daily meditation combined with developing mindfulness can result in a person experiencing more positive emotions on a daily basis. Another study published in 2014 took a group of 45 participants and made them watch clips that triggered positive emotions. The participants had no prior experience with mindfulness and were thus given a sort of "crash course" in mindfulness techniques before watching the video clips. In general, the study showed that even a brief exposure to the concept of mindfulness and the techniques surrounding it could result in a noticeable improvement in a subject's response to the positive video clips.

Why is mindfulness able to generate positive emotions? Well, the answer lies in the fact that one of the main things associated with mindfulness is emotional regulation. People who develop mindfulness get accustomed to being able to control their emotions. This makes it easier for them to suppress or get rid of negative emotions.

That right there is key.

When a person is able to keep their negative emotions in check, it only makes sense that they will experience more positive emotions.

The great news is that this doesn't take years of mindfulness to develop. In other words, no meditating on a Tibetan mountain; even a brief experience with mindfulness can lead to you developing a more positive outlook on life.

Developing a more positive outlook on life and experiencing more positive emotions can create a positive chain reaction in your life. You will start to notice that you are more motivated and focused. You will enjoy basic things like spending time with family and friends more than you used to. You will also notice that people around you respond more positively to you. You will also find that it is easier to make friends. Developing a more positive outlook on life is one of the best things that you can do for yourself and cultivating mindfulness is one of the ways of doing that.

There is a physiological factor to consider. What I mean by that is that there is evidence to suggest that developing mindfulness can actually impact your brain structure.

Yes, you can actually change how your brain is structured - for the better.

Recently, researchers have begun looking into how mindfulness and meditation can result in physiological improvements to the human body. A 2009 study took 44 participants who had a history of meditation and mindfulness. After doing physical examinations, the researchers discovered that those who meditate, and practice mindfulness actually have a larger right orbito frontal-cortex. They also had a larger right hippocampus.

What does this actually mean?

Well, those parts of your brain are responsible various functions. Most notably, they are responsible for regulating your emotions, producing positive emotions, and allowing you to exercise self-control.

Now, there need to be more studies done before we can say definitively that mindfulness actually physically changes your brain, but early studies seem to indicate that it is true. If so, this is an amazing discovery that really testifies to the power of mindfulness.

At this point you may be itching to actually learn some mindfulness techniques. Well don't worry, because I got you covered...

Interested in Building Mental Toughness?

Check out my book

"The Science of Mental Toughness:
15 Scientifically Proven Habits to Build Mental Toughness and a
High Performance Mindset"

http://a.co/gz9i58t

Chapter 4: How to Instantly Increase Attraction, Love, and Influence with People by Cultivating Mindfulness

Unless you're Darth Vader or Cruella Deville, everyone wants to be liked and accepted by others. Feeling accepted and loved by others is a deep emotional need - one that has spawned a multi-billion dollar self help industry.

Many, if not most, of you out have either heard of or read the book *How to Win Friends and Influence People* by Dale Carnegie. The famous book, which has been widely read since its release in 1936, details strategies for how to effectively interact with people. We all know the advantages that come from being likable and being able to interact with people on a positive basis. It not only helps your social life, as you can make friends more easily, but it can also help your career.

Both management and regular employees benefit from being more sociable and likable. This is especially true if you work in a field where you are expected to regularly cooperate with co-workers on big projects.

Now, what does any of this have to do with mindfulness?

Well, because the book was released so long ago (long before mindfulness was popular in the West), it does not include a section on how mindfulness and meditation can help you be more sociable and approachable. But recent scientific research has shown that cultivating mindfulness can significantly improve a person's sociability.

That is what this chapter aims to explore. In this chapter, you will learn about how mindfulness can help you make friends and influence people in the same way that any strategy from Dale Carnegie's book can.

Before we dive into some of the scientific studies that demonstrate how mindfulness can make you more sociable, we first need to talk about the connection between mindfulness and emotional intelligence.

Some of you may be familiar with the concept of emotional intelligence, mainly because it tends to be one of the things tested for on standardized tests (alongside other types of intelligence). For those unfamiliar with emotional intelligence, it essentially measures a person's ability to understand their own emotions and their ability to understand the emotions of others.

Basically, it refers to how well a person is able to understand others.

High emotional intelligence is correlated with things such as a healthy social life, good mental health, good job performance, and good leadership ability. This is important to understand because mindfulness can help you develop your emotional intelligence.

Unlike IQ which is generally static (doesn't change) emotional intelligence can be cultivated and increased. Cultivating mindfulness can help you develop your emotional intelligence.

For example, take a look at a recent 2010 study done at a Taiwanese medical school. The study took 20 graduate students and divided them into 2 groups. One group was given mindfulness training while the other group was not. After many weeks, the groups were evaluated to test whether they had experienced any improvement in their social skills and emotional intelligence. The results definitively showed that yes, mindfulness does increase one's emotional intelligence.

If one study is not enough to convince you of the power of mindfulness, there are other studies that back up these findings. A

2014 study conducted by a well-respected university in Thailand took over 300 people and analyzed their responses to a variety of survey questions that were meant analyze their familiarity with mindfulness and emotional intelligence. The results of the survey showed that *"mindfulness meditation practice tended to associate positively with emotional intelligence."* In other words, developing mindfulness leads to one developing a higher emotional intelligence.

In other words, by practicing mindfulness, you will become better and regulating your own feelings so that you can make more intelligent decisions. You'll no longer be afraid of being scared, uncomfortable, angry, or nervous - you'll get comfortable with these emotions so you can act intellectually and not emotionally.

At the same time, you'll get better at detecting other people's emotions so that you can respond to them in a way that helps you both get what you want.

That's about as close to a real-life superpower as it comes.

Moving on from emotional intelligence, there are a bunch of other ways that becoming mindful can help your social life. For starters, let's look at the idea of social connectedness. Researchers describe social connectedness as the feeling of belonging and attachment one feels when they have a steady group of friends and family.

Having a feeling of social connectedness makes you more sociable and more pleasant to be around. Mindfulness ties into this because as studies have shown, mindfulness can actually help you develop feelings of social connectedness.

For example, in a 2008 study, a group of researchers took various strangers and put them into 1 of 2 activities. One group was made to engage in activities meant to develop mindfulness while the other group was put into control group activities. The end results showed that just one session of cultivating mindfulness produced positive results for the group engaged in them. The people engaged in the mindfulness-building activities had greater feelings of social connectedness. The study also found that people were more positive towards each other after having completed the mindfulness activities.

An important part of being more sociable is learning to be more compassionate towards others and towards yourself. Compassion allows you to empathize with people more and gain a greater understanding of them. When people feel like you actually care about them, you'll be surprised what they'll do for you.

Just imagine a friend that was there for you when you needed them - wouldn't you feel a strong sense of commitment and loyalty to them?

Or imagine a spouse that supported you when no one else believed in you - wouldn't you want to show them the same level of love and dedication that they showed you?

Or how about a car salesman, who actually listened to you and your problems, taking the time to understand how you're feeling, and then sold you a car that meets your needs, not his pocketbook. Wouldn't you feel a sense to refer all of your friends and family to him?

The point is that when you show empathy and compassion - people pick up on it and want to do things for you too.

At least 2 separate studies have been done to determine whether developing mindfulness can also help others develop more compassion.

The first study was done by Stanford Medical School and it was published in 2012. The study asked participants to fill out a detailed questionnaire which measured how compassionate they were. The participants were then put through a 9-week course heavily based around cultivating mindfulness. After the 9-week course was over, they were asked to fill out the same questionnaire. The results of the study showed that in general, the participants had a reduced fear of showing compassion after they participated in the course. Likewise, the participants were also more willing to show both more compassion to others and more compassion to themselves. Finally, the study showed that people who suffer from a lack of compassion can develop it by going through courses that activities and courses that cultivate mindfulness.

These important findings are backed up by a 2013 study that also indicated that yes, individuals can become more compassionate by going through mindfulness training.

People will like you more and want to be around you more often. This will obviously make it much easier to make friends, both in your personal life and in the business world.

Let's move on now to the topic of loneliness. This could probably be its own chapter, but since we are already discussing how mindfulness can impact your social life, it makes sense to talk about it here instead of devoting an entirely separate chapter to it.

Many people experience feelings of loneliness from time to time. These feelings can actually have a very dangerous spiral effect. People feel isolated and lonely, so they do not feel confident enough to reach out and try to find friends or a significant other. Then, because they are not able to form relationships, their feelings of loneliness increase.

So, if you are one of the many people out there who suffer from persistent feelings of loneliness, then you should know that your first step should be addressing those feelings. But, how exactly should one go about addressing these feelings of loneliness? The answer is mindfulness.

Studies have shown that developing mindfulness and doing activities like meditation can actually reduce feelings of loneliness, especially in the elderly. Researchers at Carnegie Mellon University in Pennsylvania found that when people were taught mindfulness developing techniques, their feelings of isolation and loneliness actually decreased. These noticeable decreases allow people to work up the confidence to make a new friend, to ask a person out, etc.

Before ending this chapter, we should talk about one of the more interesting aspects of mindfulness, namely its ability to help reduce implicit bias and prejudice.

And in an age where racism and sexual harassment is in the news literally everyday, this is an important topic to explore here. No doubt, it's an uncomfortable issue to discuss, but it needs to be talked about.

We all have implicit biases that make socializing a bit difficult. Now, when you hear talk of biases and prejudices, your mind immediately jumps to the most well-known examples of bias and prejudice, such as racism. While that is a type of bias (and certainly a very serious one), there are other types of implicit biases that can hold you back.

For example, some people just avoid or have trouble talking to people much older or much younger than them. Others may have biases against people who dress a certain way or look a certain way. These biases can be difficult to get around and they can make socialization difficult in the workplace because you are very often forced to associate with people you would otherwise avoid.

The ability of mindfulness to reduce implicit bias was actually the subject of a few studies. In 2015 a study was published by Central Michigan University on the subject of mindfulness and implicit biases. Participants in the study engaged in activities designed to cultivate mindfulness (i.e. meditation). The study found that those who engaged in the activities had significantly less implicit race and age bias than those who did not engage in the activities. A follow-up study done later on by the same researchers confirmed that developing mindfulness does decrease a person's biases.

It may not seem that useful on the surface, but having biases can be harmful to your attempts to make friends and improve your social life. A lot of potential friendships, relationships, etc., are ruined by people's biases. So, by helping to reduce your biases, mindfulness training can actually significantly improve one's social life.

In this chapter, we have detailed how developing mindfulness can improve your social life in a variety of ways. Whether it be by increasing your emotional intelligence or by reducing your biases, developing mindfulness will make it easier for you to develop personal relationships, family relationships, and work relationships.

As was mentioned way back at the start of the chapter, developing mindfulness is easily one of the most effective ways of improving your social life and your sociability. It is certainly as effective as any strategy you will find in *How To Make Friends and Influence People*.

Chapter 5: The Foolproof Way to Build Laser Focus and Overcome Obstacles

If you've ever seen the film *Limitless*, you'll probably remember that the main character takes drugs that enhance his cognitive abilities and turn him into a super-genius (in real life, those kinds of drugs are referred to as nootropics).

Now, that film exaggerates heavily, but the underlying premise is true. Enhancing your cognitive abilities does make it easier to focus on problems and to come up with solutions. Sure, enhancing your cognitive abilities will not turn you into a genius, but it will improve your critical thinking and problem-solving skills.

Obviously, I'm not here talk to you about nootropics.

But there's a wide body of scientific evidence that suggests that mindfulness-developing activities can be helpful in boosting your various cognitive abilities (including problem-solving skills, memory skills, critical thinking ability, etc.).

As you'll see later in this chapter, these boosts in cognitive abilities apply across the age spectrum. This means that everyone, from young kids to the elderly, can benefit from becoming more mindful. This will be especially interesting to parents, looking to find ways to help their kids focus and improve in school.

Let's first start off by discussing one of the most important cognitive abilities people possess, the ability to focus your attention on a singular problem. Plenty of people have focus issues that prevent them from effectively dealing with problems. They have issues sitting down, shutting out all distractions, and focusing on a single problem.

Obviously, there are a wide range of reasons for this. They may have a very busy life with a bunch of problems demanding their attention at once (this is a very common issue for people who are balancing family and work obligations). Or it may be that they have always had issues focusing. Either way, not being able to properly focus on individual problems is a big issue. If you cannot devote all your attention to a problem, then your chances of coming up with a good solution drastically decrease. Likewise, being able to direct all your mental energy at a single issue will make it much easier to come up with a great solution.

There's lots of scientific evidence demonstrating how mindfulness can increase a person's ability to focus, so let's dig into it.

One 2007 study took 2 groups of people and asked them to participate in 2 different courses centered around developing mindfulness. The goal of the study was to find out what effect if any, mindfulness training had on the cognitive abilities of people. The results found that after an 8-week mindfulness course, the participants demonstrated improved attention spans and improved abilities to orient their attention (i.e. an improved ability to choose what they focus their attention on). The researchers theorize that this is because mindfulness enables participants to clear their mind of unnecessary distractions and focus all their attention and energy on whatever they choose. Another, more recent study published in 2010 backed up these findings. In the more recent study, researchers asked participants to go through a 4-day course on mindfulness, during which they were introduced to several mindfulness-building techniques. The results showed that even just a 4-day course on mindfulness could improve a person's attention span, their ability to process information, and their ability to remember key information.

Focus is important, but another equally important cognitive ability is memory, both short-term and long-term. It goes without saying that solving problems is difficult if you cannot recall important information. This is especially true if you are dealing with complicated or difficult problems. Improving one's short-term and long-term memory capabilities can be difficult. This is where mindfulness really shines.

Scientific research has shown that cultivating mindfulness can also improve one's ability to recall information. First off, in the last paragraph, I cited a 2010 study that, among other things, demonstrated that even a short, 4-day course on mindfulness could lead to a noticeable improvement in a person's memory abilities. Now, that was just one study, but there are others out there that back up these findings.

A study done by researchers from the University of Washington took a group of HR personnel from a company and put them into an 8-week course centered around mindfulness. The results of the study showed that, among other things, their ability to remember things was greatly improved (they also had improved multitasking abilities).

In terms of problem-solving abilities, the evidence shows that mindfulness can help with that as well. A lot of research has been done on this topic by a greatly respected Psychologist, Dr. Jonathan Schooler. He has spent much of his time at the University of California researching the connection between mindfulness and increased cognitive abilities. His research has shown that cultivating mindfulness can also boost one's ability to think critically and to problem solve.

People who develop mindfulness are more likely to think outside the box and to come up with creative solutions to problems that others might overlook. I think it goes without saying that this is an incredibly useful skill that has a wide variety of applications. Just spend a few moments thinking about how greater problem-solving skills could help you in your day-to-day life.

Don't just think about how it can help you with your career, think about how it can help you with your day-to-day life. You should be able to come up with plenty of ways that improved critical thinking and problem-solving skills can help you.

So, now that we have demonstrated that mindfulness can help increase a person's cognitive abilities, we need to turn to the question of why. Why does mindfulness seem to be able to help you improve your cognitive abilities? Well, it is a combination of 2 things.

First off, cultivating mindfulness removes stress, this is something we have covered often in this book. Getting rid of excess stress does make it a lot easier to focus and to think clearly. A little bit of stress can be good, but too much stress, and you start panicking and stop thinking clearly. Another, more important factor, has to do with the fact that cultivating mindfulness helps you use your brain's resources more efficiently. That may sound strange, but it is true. A 2007 study looked at people's ability to control their brain and determined that: "mental training can result in increased control over the distribution of limited brain resources."

What is developing mindfulness, if not a form of mental training? In the process of developing mindfulness, you learn to take total control over your body and mind, which allows you to allocate your mind's resources more effectively. This also ties into the previous point about stress.

Think of your brain as an office with a limited set of employees. When you have a lot of things to do in the office, employees get spread out and there are fewer employees working on each task, so everything gets done slower.

Now, mindfulness allows you to get rid a bunch of those tasks and refocus all your employees on one single task, which means efficiency increases. Stress is a like a task; when you are stressed out, your brain has to use resources to deal with the effects of the stress. By getting rid of the stress, resources are freed up.

Before we move onto the next chapter, we wanted to take a brief moment and talk about how this information is also useful for younger kids and teenagers. Adults are not the only ones who benefit from cognitive improvements; kids in school can benefit just as much as adults.

For example, a recent 2016 study asked a group of elementary students to participate in mindfulness training. The results of the study showed that the mindfulness training resulted in greater academic performance for the students. Another study also showed that mindfulness training helped children with learning disorders (specifically ADHD) to focus on their academics, which led to an improvement in their academic performance. One of the main reasons that mindfulness is so useful for kids and teenagers is that it helps them get over academic related stress, which, when combined with the improvements in their cognitive abilities, results in greater academic achievement.

In this chapter, we have focused on how mindfulness training can actually help you improve your ability to think. Now, it is worth stating again that mindfulness training will not turn you into a genius overnight.

However, the evidence is clear that when you develop mindfulness, you gain greater critical thinking, problem solving, and memory abilities which are extremely helpful in a number of situations. Usually, to get this sort of cognitive improvement, people have to resort to nootropics, which can be dangerous. With mindfulness training, you can achieve the same sort of improved cognitive abilities, all without taking a single pill; pretty impressive if you ask me.

Interested in Developing Your Power of Focus?

Check out my book,

"**30 Days of Focus**: The Step by Step Guide to Supercharge Your Productivity and Crush Your Goals in the Next 30 Days"

http://a.co/7IGcbZU

Chapter 6: How to Win at Work and Become More Productive Using Mindfulness

Most of the benefits of mindfulness will help you in your personal life, from your health, to your ability to influence people, to your cognitive abilities. But it could also be applied to the workplace and your professional life.

For example, think back to the early chapter on how mindfulness can help combat stress; it is easy to see how that chapter could easily be applied to the workplace. After all, workplace stress is a major issue and it makes sense that doing something to reduce the stress of individual employees would help make the workplace as a whole more efficient.

Despite this, it's worthwhile to dedicate an entire chapter to how mindfulness can be used in the workplace. The workplace is one of the areas where developing mindfulness is the most useful and there have been a lot of interesting studies looking at what happens when mindfulness-building techniques are introduced to workplaces.

This chapter will be useful for both employees and management alike. For employees, this chapter will further show just how useful mindfulness can be. For those in management positions, this chapter will show them how mindfulness can be used to make their workplace and employees better.

For starters, mindfulness can be very helpful in improving one's "executive functions." For those who are unfamiliar with what executive functions are, they refer to a set of specific things that your brain does; specifically, it refers to the tools your brain uses to take in information and formulate a response to it. So, how would this translate to a workplace?

Well, exposing employees to mindfulness training will improve their ability to absorb information and to come up with an appropriate response to that information. It goes without saying that increasing your employees' ability to absorb and process important information is extremely useful.

Likewise, increasing their ability to formulate responses to that information will result in more creative and more effective solutions to obstacles.

Now, you will recall that this was touched on in chapter 5 when I talked about how mindfulness can help increase a person's ability to problem solve and to think outside the box, so I will not spend too much time on this topic. However, I do want to re-emphasize that introducing mindfulness is a great way to have people take a fresh look problems.

Let's talk about employee stress and burnout, it is an issue that plagues every industry. It doesn't matter if the employees are working in the service industry, working in an office, or working as contractors, stress impacts every employee negatively.

For an employer, one of the worst things that can happen is that your employees become burned out and unsatisfied with their job, this results in subpar performance from employees.

From an employee's perspective, being burned out at work is a terrible feeling. The stress and exhaustion that stem from being dissatisfied with one's job bleed into other parts of one's life.

The good news is that mindfulness can address all the issues related to burnout. It may sound too good to be true, but it is 100% true and backed up by scientific studies. As you will see, developing mindfulness can make you feel more satisfied with your work and reduce feelings of burnout.

In 2013, the Tavistock Institute, a British non-profit organization dedicated to researching topics related to workplace behavior, published a report on service workers and workplace mindfulness. The report had 2 very important pieces of information in it. Firstly, service workers who were given mindfulness training had more vigor and energy when doing their jobs. Secondly, after being given mindfulness training, service workers were also found to be more dedicated to their work. The service industry can be a very stressful and exhausting line of work, so it is a testament to the effectiveness of mindfulness that it is able to help service workers avoid burnout.

Other, more recent scientific studies have backed up these findings. A 2016 study found that mindfulness helps workers create "buffers" between their work and their personal lives that helps prevent burnout.

A major cause of burnout is the stress of work bleeding into a worker's personal life. Some people are able to leave the stress behind at the office when they clock out, but others do not have the same luxury. It is the latter that is most at risk of suffering from burnout.

Mindfulness lets these workers clear their minds of any work-related stress and it lets them have more control over their minds, which allows them to block out work-related issues and focus on other, less stressful things. Even more interestingly, studies have also shown that when employees are given mindfulness training, their desire to leave the company they are working for decreases significantly. This suggests that mindfulness can be useful for workplaces or businesses that have high employee turnover, or that want to increase their chances of maintaining key employees.

Finally, let's talk about one of the most interesting things that researchers have discovered recently about how mindfulness can impact employees. A 2017 study found that when employees were given mindfulness training, the employees were more willing to work more contract hours. Now, these findings will not be of any great interest to employees, but if you are in a management position or if you own a business, then these findings should be of great interest to you. When combined with the other effects of mindfulness training (decreased workplace stress, decreased burnout, and increased cognitive abilities), it adds up to a drastic increase in workplace efficiency.

As this chapter has demonstrated, there are a lot of workplace benefits associated with mindfulness. The benefits are just not restricted to either employees or people in a management/ownership position either. Employees who feel they are on the brink of burnout or who want to improve their performance at their job can consider looking into mindfulness. Likewise, managers or business owners looking to build a more stress-free and effective workplace can consider looking into mindfulness training for their employees. It is for these reasons that many major companies have begun looking into mindfulness and MBSR for their workplaces.

Chapter 7: Six Simple Exercises You Can Do to Develop Mindfulness

So far, this entire book has been dedicated to 2 distinct topics, defining mindfulness and explaining the benefits of it.

However, you may have noticed that something is missing.

Namely, we have not yet discussed how one should actually go about developing mindfulness. It is all well and good to talk about the benefits of mindfulness, but if you don't know how to actually make yourself more mindful, then it is not really all that useful, is it?

In some of the chapters in this book, we talked about people being put through professionally created mindfulness training courses. This might give you the idea that in order to start developing mindfulness, that you need to engage the services of a professional or participate in a professionally designed course.

Neither of these is true. In fact, you can start developing mindfulness on your own.

All you need is a helpful guide that can give you step-by-step instructions on how to do mindfulness building exercises. As you can probably guess from the title, that is the purpose of this chapter.

I am going to give you a list of exercises that you can do on your own to start developing mindfulness. These aren't just exercises that I have come up with, these are exercises used by researchers in many of the studies that have been mentioned all throughout this book. If you want a particular example, many of these exercises were used in a 2007 study done by researchers Jan Fleming and Nancy Kocovski to determine if mindfulness could be used to help with social anxiety.

Exercise 1: The Food Exercise

Alright, so the first exercise want to discuss is a good exercise for beginners. So, if you want to completely start from the beginning (which is what I recommend), then this is that exercise you should start doing first.

It's called the "food exercise" because you can do it with any food that you want. Typically, most people will do it with a raisin, and thus it gets commonly referred to as the "raisin exercise." But, rest assured you can use pretty much any food item with this exercise (although, something that does not cause a mess and that is relatively small works the best).

In this exercise, you take a whatever piece of food you have chosen and hold it in your hand. Now, in professional mindfulness courses, participants will be asked to forget everything they know about the particular food item they have chosen. They will be asked to forget what it smells like, what it feels like, what it looks like, and what it tastes like. Now, this can be difficult to do on your own, but if you really put effort into it, then you should be able to accomplish this.

Once you have forgotten everything you know about your food item, you should pick it up and start inspecting it. Note everything about it. Note how it smells, how it feels, how heavy it is, how it looks, and how it tastes.

It may sound silly (and it will probably look silly doing it), but there is logic behind it. By forgetting everything you know and the relearning it, you are forcing your mind to drop everything else and focus on the particular item you picked up. It forces your mind into the here and now.

This exercise alone does not necessarily build mindfulness, but it teaches you a skill that is very important; namely, the ability to clear your mind and focus on something in front of you.

Without this skill, developing mindfulness and doing other mindfulness exercises will be more difficult. This is why the exercise is perfect for beginners, it sets up a foundation that you can build off in future mindfulness-building exercises.

Exercise 2: Body Scanning

If you will recall, we talked a bit about body scanning in the introduction to this book, so some of you may recognize this term. However, if you do not remember, or if you skipped the introduction, fear not, because in this section we will be explaining what body scanning is in greater detail.

Body scanning as an exercise is very similar to the previous exercise in that both force you to clear your mind and focus on one specific thing in front of you. The main difference is that body scanning is a lot more advanced and a lot more useful for building mindfulness.

A typical body scan follows roughly 4 steps:

First off, you get into a comfortable position. Generally, the 2 positions recommended by experts include laying on your back looking upwards or sitting on a comfortable chair, with your back straight and your feet firmly planted on the ground. The most important thing is that you are comfortable with the way that you are sitting.

Secondly, you need to go completely still for a few moments and try to shake off any lingering thoughts that are not related to the exercise. This step can range from a minute to 10 minutes depending on your current state of mind. Length does not matter; so, feel free to take as long as you want on this step. If you notice that the step is taking a lot longer than you would like, don't sweat it, you'll get better at it as you become more mindful.

Thirdly, you need to start focusing on your breathing. Think about what you do when you're trying to calm someone down, you tell them to breathe in and out slowly. You should do the same thing, but make sure that you focus on your breaths. Think about the rhythm of breathing, think about the process of breathing in and breathing out, etc.

Finally, you need to start thinking about the individual parts of your body. Think about them in the same way that you thought about the food item in the previous exercise. Pretend you know nothing about your body and slowly start relearning each part of it. Think about how each part of your body feels, think about how it feels when pressed against clothing or when exposed to the air.

Typically, experts will tell people to start at the bottom of their body, with their toes, and then work their way upwards. Keep moving until you reach your head and then stop. Slowly exit a body scan, you do not want to move too fast, otherwise, you will disrupt the calm that has been brought on by the body scan.

Exercise 3: Mindful Gazing

This exercise is, in my opinion, one of the more interesting mindfulness-building exercises that one can do. Simply go outside and find a nice, quiet space to sit down. Alternatively, if you cannot do that (because you cannot find a quiet space) try finding a window in your house with a nice view and sit down there. The next step is very simple, just start looking at things and thinking about them.

But here is the thing, you cannot just label things. "Why?" you may ask. Well, if you label things, then you really are not focusing on them. So, if you see a bird and think to yourself "there's a bird," your mind just accepts that and moves on. This is not mindfulness. So, what you should do instead is think about individual parts of what you see.

For example, if you see a bird, do not think to yourself "that's a bird." Instead, think about its colors, how its wings work, how it sounds, and other information like that. This forces your mind to think about those individual parts and focus on them, which is what mindfulness is.

This exercise is pretty versatile in that you can look at anything you want. You can also do it for as long as you want. You can do it for 5 minutes or for 50 minutes, it doesn't matter. Even doing it for a small amount of time can be useful.

Exercise 4: Mindful Listening

It's safe to say that most of us like listening to music, but how well do we really listen? A lot of us just hum the words or we just keep the music on in the background while doing something else.

There's nothing wrong with any of this, but you can use music to help you develop mindfulness. That is the purpose of this exercise, to use music to help you become more mindful. This exercise technically doesn't require anything aside from music, but it works best if you have some sort of way of listening to music more closely (i.e. a good sound system or a good pair of headphones). But, if you don't, don't worry, you can still do this exercise by listening to music on your computer or by putting on a CD.

The goal of this exercise is to break down the music and focus on its individual parts. Start by focusing in on the beat of the song. You may also want to focus on individual instruments like the drums or the guitar. Then focus on the lyrics, think about how they sound and what they mean.

It's also important that you leave behind any preconceived notions about the music that you are listening to. A lot of people associate particular songs with certain emotions or memories. A song may trigger happy memories, sad memories, or some mixture of the 2. While this isn't a bad thing, it can hinder your attempts to build mindfulness. Thus, it is best to either pick a song that doesn't trigger any memories or to leave your memories at the door when doing the exercise.

Exercise 5: On The Spot Mindfulness

This exercise differs greatly from the last 4 in that it doesn't require any preparation. As you can tell from the title, this exercise is meant to be done on the spot, when things are getting hectic. In a way, it combines many of the aspects from the previous exercises.

If you ever notice you're in a stressful or panicked environment, try and find a quiet moment. Once you have a moment, start thinking about the various emotions that you are feeling. Do not think about changing them, just acknowledge them and note why you feel those particular emotions.

After that, start thinking about other things, do a quick body scan, or focus on something in the room. Do a breathing exercise and focus on your breathing. No matter what you end up doing, you want to do something that helps you clear your mind and reorient yourself.

The idea behind this exercise is to help you clear your head quickly when you are in a stressful situation. The other exercises require a bit more preparation and time, the advantage of this exercise is that you only need a quiet moment to yourself.

So, if you are at work or on the go, you can do this exercise quickly to reorient yourself.

Exercise 6: Mindful Activities
We all have to do basic household chores, such as washing dishes, cleaning the house, cleaning the car, etc. Normally, these chores are boring and uneventful, but they need to be done, so we suffer through them.

However, these chores actually provide a good opportunity to build mindfulness. The idea behind this exercise is to really pay attention to the activity that you are doing. Typically, we tend to blank out when we are doing these activities or chores because they're boring, and we want to get them over with.

However, when doing this exercise actually focus on the activity you are doing. If you are cleaning your house, focus on the little things. Think about the muscles you are using while doing the activity. Think about why you are cleaning the house. The ultimate goal is to immerse yourself in the activity that you are doing and to really focus on it. This exercise can also be applied to work-related activities as well.

Chapter 8: Meditation: The Best Way To Develop Mindfulness

"I mean the whole thing about meditation and yoga is about connecting to the higher part of yourself, and then seeing that every living thing is connected in some way."

Most of you will probably know about Hollywood star Gillian Anderson from her time on the hit television show, *The X-Files*, but most of you probably are not aware that she is a big supporter of regular meditation. She's not the only one either.

Countless numbers of great thinkers, actors, actresses, athletes, great leaders, CEOs, and other famous and successful people regularly meditate. You may be asking "why." Well, the answer is quite simple, meditation helps you in a variety of ways.

It's been scientifically proven to help reduce stress, reduce anxiety, help you focus, make you more productive, and that's just the tip of the iceberg when it comes to the benefits of meditation.

I have talked a lot in this book about mindfulness. While that is the main focus of the book, as was mentioned in the introduction, one of the key ways of cultivating mindfulness is through calming activities like meditation.

Technically meditation is simply another activity that you can do to develop mindfulness; so, I should have included it in the previous chapter. But, meditation is so deep and so connected to developing mindfulness, that I felt it was worthy of its own, in-depth chapter.

The purpose of this chapter is to introduce the practice of meditation, which is so intimately connected with mindfulness. For example, Jon

Kabat-Zinn, who you will remember as being very influential in the development of mindfulness, meditates daily because, in his view, it is necessary for developing mindfulness.

When people think of "meditation" they think of Buddhist monks sitting cross-legged and humming to themselves. While that is a perfectly valid way to meditate, meditation is a lot more complex than it looks and there are many different ways to meditate.

Meditation is an ancient practice, with some historians saying it can be traced back to 2600 BC (that would make meditation at least 4000 years old).

In that time, many different styles and forms of meditation have been developed. To help you get into meditation, we are going to spend the rest of this introduction explaining the basics of meditation and what you need to do to start meditating on a daily basis.

What you need to start meditating

Before we start going over how to meditate, we are first going to cover things that you need to get before you can start meditating.

A quiet room

This is both the most important and the hardest thing to acquire depending on your living situation. In order to meditate properly, you need to remove yourself from all distractions. That means you need to be away from ambient noise (such as televisions, air conditioners, etc.) you also need to be away from others.

So, if you have kids or others living in the house with you, you need to make sure they are not constantly interrupting your meditation. For some, getting a quiet room to meditate in will be easier than it is for others. Some will have the luxury of being able to make an entire room dedicated to meditation, others will not have that same luxury.

The most important things to look for when creating a meditation room are to make sure that it is uncluttered and that it is able to be shut off from other parts of your home. So, you do not want to choose a room that people have to walk through to get to other parts of the home. At the same time, you do not want to pick a place like a bedroom, because those tend to have beds and furniture in them that make the spaces too cluttered for meditation. A garage can be an ideal place for a meditation room, assuming that it is not too cluttered. Another good place may be a basement, but again, this depends on the state of your basement. If money is not an issue, you can always look into renting a meditation room, but this is not essential.

With a bit of work, everyone should be able to make at least one room in their home into a suitable meditation space.

Something comfortable to sit on

Going back to what I said earlier, when most people think of meditating, they think of a Buddhist monk sitting cross-legged on the floor. But, it is actually recommended that you sit on something while meditating. There are a few reasons for this.

Firstly, meditation can be a long process and sitting on the ground for extended periods of time can be bad for your lower back (this is especially true if you are older and if you have had back problems in the past).

Secondly, an important part of meditation is maintaining correct posture. You need to be sitting completely straight while meditating. A lot of people slouch when they sit on the ground, so sitting on something can help you keep correct posture during the entire session. Most experts will recommend a meditation cushion. As the name suggests, this is a small, comfortable cushion that you sit on while meditating. They are cheap and can be found in plenty of physical stores and on Amazon. If you want something bigger, you can buy chairs and benches that are meant for meditation exclusively. Benches and chairs are good for taller people, who may not be able to sit properly on a cushion.

A timer

A small, but important part of meditation involves proper time-keeping. It is important that you meditate for a consistent amount of time each day and it can be difficult to keep track of time on your own. A timer can be very helpful in ensuring that you meditate for the exact same amount of time each day.

There are plenty of free apps that you can get for your phone that will keep track of the time for you (most also keep track of other useful information, such as how many sessions you have completed). The only issue with using your phone is that there is a possibility that you will be distracted by your phone (texts, calls, etc.).

You may also be distracted by the temptation to look at your phone while meditating. Because of this, some people find it helpful to buy a small, regular timer.

How to meditate properly

Now that you have everything you need, you can start meditating properly.

Sit properly

The first thing you want to do when meditating is get into a proper sitting position. Take your cushion, chair, or bench and sit down. If you are sitting on a cushion, then cross your legs, this will help you maintain proper posture. You want to make sure that you are "sitting tall." What that means is that you are sitting completely straight.

For some people, this can be difficult because their natural inclination is to slouch. If you are having trouble sitting straight, close your eyes and visualize a long piece of string running from the very top of your head to the bottom of your back. Now imagine it pulling your back straight up. Keep this image in the back of your mind and you will find it easier to sit up straight continually.

Begin relaxing your body

Once you have your posture correct, focus on relaxing your body. And when I say, "relaxing your body" I mean every muscle. You need to become as relaxed as possible, otherwise, you will not be getting the full value from meditation. You need to release all the tension in every part of your body. Start from one part of your body and work your way up or down.

Sit in silence

After your body is completely relaxed, take a few moments and just sit in silence. Try not to think about anyone or anything. Just be still and sit in silence. The purpose of this step is to ensure that any remaining tension or thoughts are gone from your mind. Only when your body and mind are completely relaxed can you move onto the next step.

Begin breathing

After a few moments of silence, you can start focusing on your breathing. Start breathing deeply in and deeply out. Now, you do not have to exaggerate your breaths like you do when you are at the doctor's office. Just breathe normally, but make sure you go slowly. Breathe in through your nose and out through your mouth.

Start saying your mantra

A mantra is a word or a set of words that you can say to yourself while meditating. You can find lists of mantras online, but I would encourage you to develop your own because a mantra is an incredibly personal thing and it will have the most impact if you use one you came up with. A mantra should be short and to the point.

For example, someone meditating to reduce stress should say something that reinforces the fact that they can get through stressful times (they may say something like "I am a rock" over and over again). You should repeat the mantra at a steady pace.

One thing I like to do is imagine that I am who or what I want to be. I put myself in their body, and see the world through their eyes. I talk to myself like they would talk to themselves and imagine myself acting like them.

When I do this, I feel an incredible sense of calm, and excitement. I know they're opposite emotions, but it's hard to describe. It's almost like the feeling of flying, I get excited, but am calm and placid at the same time.

Often times I have my biggest breakthroughs and inspirational moments when I'm meditating like this.

End the session

Ending a meditation session is just as important as starting it. Ending a meditation session should be done slowly. You should not just spring up and go on with your day. Instead, slowly open your eyes and readjust yourself. Look at various things in your meditation room. Next, start moving your feet and hands, as they may be a bit stiff. Start thinking what you need to do for the rest of the day, this will get your mind working again. Once you feel grounded again, you can end your session and pack up everything.

Meditation and Mindfulness, the keys to a happy life

Now that you understand how to meditate properly, you can begin to use meditation to help you cultivate mindfulness. Think of meditation and mindfulness as being the two keys to living a happy, fulfilling life. While there are certainly other ways of developing mindfulness, meditation is one of the best methods for doing so and it is recommended that you at least give it a try.

Conclusion

In this book, you have been introduced to the concept of mindfulness, you have been introduced to various studies proving the benefits of mindfulness, and you have been introduced to exercises that can help you build mindfulness. So, there is only one more thing that needs to be discussed, and that is how to continue your education in mindfulness. This book is meant to lay a solid foundation from which you can build off. I gave you a list of good exercises, such as meditation, which can help you build mindfulness. But, there is much more out there to discover when it comes to mindfulness. This book should be treated as a starting guide. It is meant to introduce you to the concept of mindfulness and get you familiar with it. You would be letting yourself down if you stopped exploring mindfulness after finishing this book. As I hope all of you understand by now, there are enormous benefits associated with developing mindfulness, and there are likely many more benefits yet to be discovered. So, it would be a bad idea for you to stop exploring mindfulness now; given that you know about the huge amount of benefits associated with it.

So, use this book to help ease yourself into the world of mindfulness. Start doing some of the exercises. Read some of the studies that I have mentioned for yourself. But do not stop there.

Read more articles from experts, read other books, look to see if you can find mindfulness courses being offered in your area. If possible, introduce your family and friends to the concept. The most important thing is that you continue learning about mindfulness.

The process of developing mindfulness is a long one, and I hope that this book has provided you with the tools and knowledge necessary to start that journey.

Here's What To Do Next

I hope you enjoyed this book.

But more than that I hope that you **take action.**

Things don't happen by themselves and you're the only one that's responsible for your situation in life.

If you want to live your life to its fullest potential, you need to find focus, discipline, and practice a tremendous amount of self discipline. The good news is by simply using the clear cut instructions and tips in this book, you can get quick, effective, and powerful results. I wish you nothing but the best success.

I really want to help you achieve your goals, and if you read this book and do the exercises for the next 30 days, I'm sure that you'll develop the mindfulness, serenity, and peace of mind you want.

If you have a question that you need help with, email me at razasimam@outlook.com and I'll personally do what I can to help you get on track.

Please Leave a Review – It's Means a Lot

I hope you enjoyed this book. If you did, please leave me a review. It will only take 30 seconds and it would mean a LOT to me as an author.

We live and die by reviews.

- They help us know how our readers feel about our work
- They give us the motivation to keep writing
- They help others learn about our books

So please leave a review now.

Thanks in advance ☺

Made in the USA
Columbia, SC
14 November 2018